MATERIALS *and* MATTER

MAKING SENSE *of* SCIENCE

Peter Riley

W

FRANKLIN WATTS
LONDON•SYDNEY

First published in 2005 by Franklin Watts
96 Leonard Street, London EC2A 4XD

Franklin Watts Australia
45–51 Huntley Street, Alexandria, NSW 2015

Series Editor: Rachel Cooke
Editors: Kate Newport and Andrew Solway
Art director: Jonathan Hair
Designer: Mo Choy

Picture credits:

Dr Jeremy Burgess/Science Photo Library: 23c. Mark Edwards/Still
Pictures: front cover main, 1. Firepix/Topham: 13t, 18. Simon Fraser/
Science Photo Library: 29b. Bob Krist/Corbis: 25br. Imagestate/Alamy: 4.
Andrew Lambert Photographs/Science Photo Library: 15cl. MSP/Topham:
11b. Novosti/Science Photo Library: 15tr. Picturepoint/Topham: 17, 19b,
26t, 27c, 28, 29t. Red Blue Green New Media Ltd/Alamy: front cover insert.
Science Photo Library: 25tr. Mitch Wojnarowicz/Image Works/Topham: 14t.

Every attempt has been made to clear copyright. Should there be any
inadvertent omission please apply to the publisher for rectification.

Picture research: Diana Morris

All other photography by Ray Moller.

Every attempt has been made to clear copyright.
Should there be any inadvertent omission,
please apply to the publisher for rectification.

A CIP catalogue record for this book
is available from the British Library.

ISBN 0 7496 5529 1

Printed in Malaysia

CONTENTS

MATERIAL WORLD

Many people think of material as being pieces of cloth. It is true that cloth is a material, but wood, metal, pottery and plastic are materials too. And the list does not end there. Water, blood and oil are also materials. The air we breathe, the gas people use for cooking, the scents we smell – all these are materials. In fact, everything around us is a material of some kind. A material is anything made from the 'stuff' that scientists call matter.

The only place where there is no material is in space. Between the stars and the galaxies there is truly empty space, which contains no matter at all.

Every material on Earth takes one of three forms: it is a solid, a liquid or a gas. Solids are things with definite shapes, such as houses, trees and books. Liquids, such as water and cooking oil, have no definite shape: they change and flow. Gases are less easy to notice because most of them are invisible. However, we can feel wind, which is the movement of the gases in air, and we can smell the exhaust gases that come from a car. Solid, liquid and gas are called the three states of matter.

DIFFERENT PROPERTIES

The things that make materials different from each other are their properties. One property of a solid material is how hard it is. A rock, for example, is hard, while a sponge is soft. Liquids can differ in viscosity: this means how runny they are. Honey and treacle are highly viscous – they flow very slowly – while water, with a low viscosity, flows easily. Most gases, such as oxygen and carbon dioxide, are colourless. However, chlorine (a gas used to make disinfectants) is green.

CHOOSING MATERIALS

For about two million years, people have been taking natural materials and adapting them for their own uses. We use materials with different properties for different purposes. For example, we twist together strands of wool from a sheep to form woollen yarn, then weave or knit the yarn to make clothes that are comfortable and keep us warm.

Wool would be a very poor material for a drink container. But if we moisten clay, mould it, then heat it to very high temperatures in a kiln, it makes a hard, waterproof kind of pottery called stoneware — perfect for a coffee mug!

MAKE A BADGE FROM MILK

Alchemists (see the panel below) often warmed and mixed substances to make changes happen. These processes have been a part of chemistry for hundreds of years.

Ask an adult to heat about a third of litre of milk for you. It must not boil. Add a tablespoon of vinegar and stir. When white lumps appear, separate them from the liquid with a sieve. Squash the lumps together in the sieve to squeeze out more liquid, then form the lump into a disc. Push a safety pin part-way into one side of the disc, and leave it to set. Paint a design on your badge once it has dried.

REAL-LIFE WIZARDS?

One of the first groups of people to study in detail the properties of materials and how they can be changed were alchemists. Alchemy began in Ancient Egypt over 2,000 years ago. Alchemists had two aims: they wanted to change ordinary metals into gold, and to make a medicine that could give everlasting life. No alchemists managed to do either of these things, but some of their observations and experiments became part of the science of chemistry, which first developed about 400 years ago.

WHAT IS MATTER?

Tap your head – it is solid matter. Feel your pulse – blood (liquid matter) is being pushed through your body. Breathe in and out – feel the air (gaseous matter) moving in your airways. We are made of matter and we live in a material world.

It is difficult to think what matter really is – there is so much of it! But all matter has two things in common. Matter has mass, and it takes up space.

MASS AND WEIGHT

The mass of an object is the amount of matter it contains. The Earth's gravity pulls on this mass, with a force called weight. We can feel the weight of solid objects by picking them up (if they are not too heavy!), and we can feel the weight of a liquid by comparing a full glass with an empty one. Gases do not seem to have weight, but a simple experiment can show that air has weight and therefore also mass.

BALLOON BALANCE

Tie two similar-sized balloons to the ends of a metre rule and hang the rule so that it balances. Now take one of the balloons off, blow it up and put it back on the rule. The rule will no longer balance, because of the weight of the air in the inflated balloon.

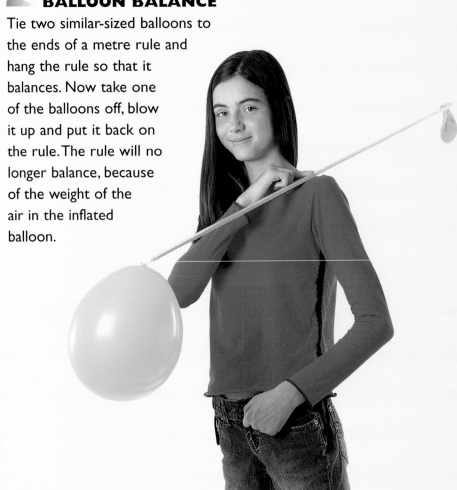

VOLUME

The space taken up by matter is called its volume. You can work out the volume of a solid, rectangular block of matter by multiplying its length by its width and height. So a block of wood 2 centimetres long, 3 centimetres wide and 4 centimetres high, has a volume of 24 cubic centimetres (24 cm^3). A liquid has no shape, but you can find the volume of a liquid by pouring it into a measuring cylinder or beaker. To measure the volume of a gas, you can suck it into a syringe.

Using a ruler, a measuring beaker and a syringe, you can measure the volume of a solid, a liquid and a gas.

THE VOLUME OF A PEBBLE

You can use a measuring cylinder to find the volume of an irregular solid object, such as a pebble. Half fill a measuring cylinder with water and note the volume. Drop in a pebble, and note the volume again. The pebble's volume is the difference between these two volumes.

DENSITY

The density of a material is a property that combines mass and volume. It is a measure of the mass of a substance in a certain volume. For instance, if a 24 cm³ block of cork has a mass of 6 grams (6 g), it has a density of (6 ÷ 24) = 0.25 g/cm³.

SEPARATING THE STATES

The properties of volume and density are important in distinguishing between solids, liquids and gases.
• Solids have a high density and their volume does not change. They have a definite shape.
• Liquids have a high density and their volume does not change, but they have no definite shape. Liquids take up the shape of whatever container they are in.
• Gases have a low density and their volume can vary. Gases have no definite shape – they completely fill whatever container they are in.

The volume and density of a solid or a liquid does not change. The volume of a gas can vary – and with it its density. Air forced into a balloon is more dense than the air around the balloon.

THE **FOUR ELEMENTS**

Thales (642–546 BC), a Greek philosopher, believed that all matter was really different forms of a single substance. He called this substance an element. Later, the Greek philosopher Empedocles (about 490–430 BC) stated that matter was made from four elements – air, earth, fire and water. Different substances were mixtures of different amounts of these four elements. Alchemists used the idea of the four elements in their studies of matter.

PARTICLES OF MATTER

What would you get if you took a piece of cheese and cut it in two, then cut one half in two again, and then one half of that in two and so on? This idea of cutting something up occurred to the ancient Greek philosopher Democritus (470–380 BC). He came to the conclusion that, if you kept on cutting, you would reach a particle so small that it could not be divided. He called this particle an atom, which means indivisible.

This picture shows the different kinds of atoms and molecules found in air.

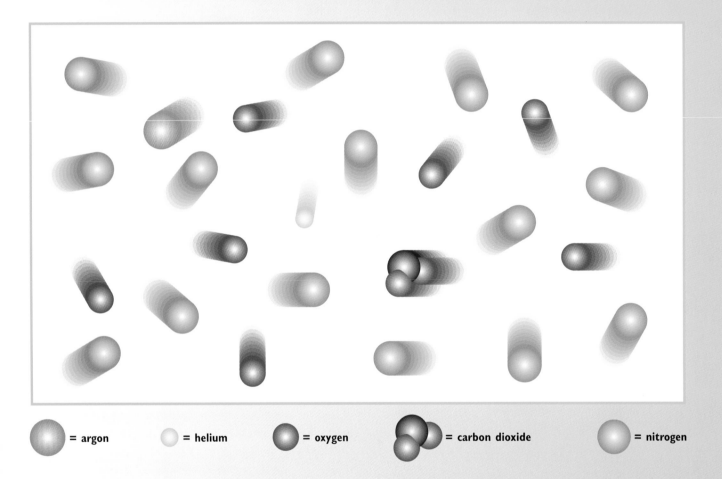

= argon   = helium   = oxygen   = carbon dioxide   = nitrogen

Today we know from the work of many scientists that matter is really made up of tiny particles. The smallest of them are atoms, but there are also other particles called molecules, made from groups of atoms. All matter is made from atoms or from molecules. Some materials are made from just atoms and some are made from just molecules. Other substances, such as air, are mixtures of different materials and contain both atoms and molecules.

ON THE WAY TO AN ATOM

Take a piece of paper and tear it in two. Take one of the halves and tear it in two. Tear one of the new pieces in two. Keep tearing the paper in this way until the pieces are too small to tear. Atoms are still much smaller than this. There are millions of them in the ink of the full stop at the end of this sentence.

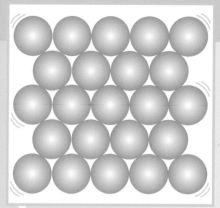

particles in a solid

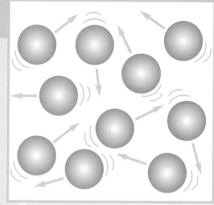

particles in a liquid

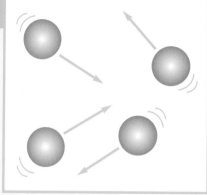

particles in a gas

PARTICLES IN MATTER

The particles in matter help to explain the properties of solids, liquids and gases.

In solids, the atoms or molecules are packed together tightly. There is very little space between them so the solid cannot be squashed. The particles hold tightly to each other, so the solid keeps its shape. Even though the particles are held in a rigid structure, they do vibrate a little.

The particles in liquids are close together so, like solids, liquids cannot be compressed. However, the particles are not fixed together but can slide over each other. This allows a liquid to flow. It also means that a liquid does not have a fixed shape. The particles simply flow until they come up against the wall of a container. Then they take up the shape of the container.

The particles in a gas do not hold on to each other in any way. They zoom about in all directions. A gas will fill any container it is in. When the container is large, the particles are far apart, but the gas can be squashed, like the air in a bicycle tyre, so that the particles come closer together.

PEAS AS PARTICLES

Tightly pack some frozen peas into the lid of a coffee jar. The peas are like the particles in a solid. Now take some peas out and tip the lid a little so that the peas can flow like particles in a liquid. Remove most of the peas and gently shake the lid from side to side. The remaining peas move quickly in all directions like the particles in a gas.

THE PARTICLES THEORY OF MATTER

The idea of matter being made from particles was developed from the study of gases. James Clerk Maxwell (1831–1879) and Ludwig Boltzmann (1844–1906) studied the results of experiments on gases done by many scientists. They found that the behaviour of gases could be explained if they were thought of as being made from tiny, fast-moving particles. Since gases can turn into liquids or solids (see pages 10–11), these too must be made of particles.

PHYSICAL CHANGES

Have you ever put a piece of chocolate in your pocket and forgotten about it? In time, the heat from your body makes it change from a solid to a sticky liquid! If you put the melted chocolate in a cool place, it turns back to a solid again. These changes show that matter can change its state.

Changes in state are called physical changes. These changes are reversible, as we saw with the chocolate.

Material	Melting/freezing point (°C)
water	0
butter	about 33
chocolate	about 37
candle wax	about 60
nylon	about 250
lead	327
gold	1064
glass	about 1500
iron	1538

This table shows the melting or freezing points of some common materials.

PARTICLES IN PHYSICAL CHANGES

The particles in a solid have a little energy, which makes them vibrate. When a solid is heated, it receives more energy, which makes the particles vibrate more. If the particles receive enough energy, they vibrate so much that they break free and slide over each other. This process is called melting. The temperature at which this takes place is the melting point of the solid.

As a liquid cools down, it loses energy. At a certain point, the particles lose so much energy that they can no longer slide over each other: they cling to other particles and vibrate. This is what happens when a liquid freezes. We usually think of freezing as something that happens at low temperatures, as when water freezes. But candle wax, for instance, freezes when it is still warm to the touch. The freezing point of a material is the same as its melting point.

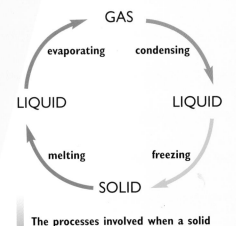

The processes involved when a solid changes to a liquid, then a gas, then back to a solid again.

EVAPORATION

During a rain shower puddles develop, but they do not stay long once the sun comes out. The water disappears by changing from a liquid to a gas – a process called evaporation.

The particles in a liquid slide over each other, but there is still an attraction between the particles that holds them together. However, particles at the surface are held in place only by the liquid particles below them. If the surface particles are moving fast enough, they can break away and form a gas.

HOW FAST DOES WATER EVAPORATE?

Put a saucer of water on a sunny window-sill. Mark the level of the water. After an hour, mark the new water level. Check and record the water level at other times over the next day. Predict when it will all have evaporated and see if you are right.

BOILING

When a liquid is heated, many particles evaporate from the surface. But particles within the liquid get enough energy to evaporate too. These high-energy particles collect together to form bubbles of gas, which rise to the surface and pop. When a liquid boils, it is constantly being stirred up by large gas bubbles forming and popping.

CONDENSATION

Condensation is the reverse of evaporation – a gas cools down and turns to liquid. You can see condensation happening if you breathe on a can of cold drink from the fridge. Droplets of water form on the can as the water vapour in your warm breath condenses on its cold surface.

DRAMATIC SMOKE

If you have been to a pop concert, you may have seen the effect of another physical change. It is called sublimation and it occurs when a solid turns directly into a gas. Dry ice is solid carbon dioxide. When it is exposed to the air, the solid immediately changes to a gas. Energy is used up in this process, and the air becomes colder. Water vapour in the cold air condenses to make clouds that look like smoke.

The 'smoke' at this pop concert is actually a cloud of tiny water droplets produced by releasing dry ice.

MIXTURES AND SOLUTIONS

If you get a whiff of perfume, or smell newly cut grass, you are smelling something mixed in with the air. Small amounts of perfume, or chemicals from the cut grass, evaporate and mix with the gases in the air. When the scent chemicals reach your nose, you smell them.

Air itself is made up of several different gases, as we saw on page 8. When different substances mingle together they form a mixture. The process of one substance mingling and spreading out through another is called diffusion.

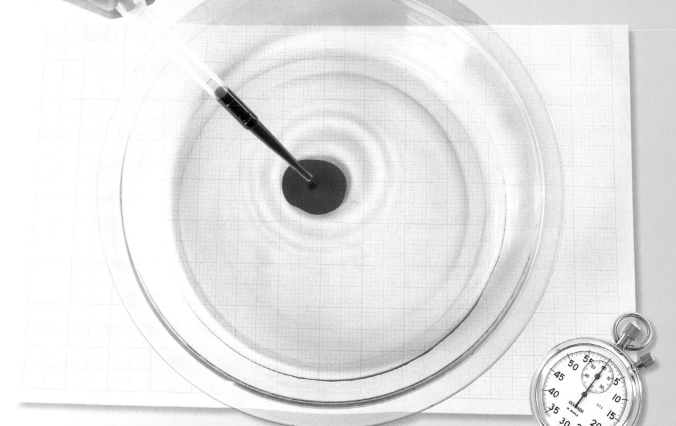

WATCHING DIFFUSION

Watch diffusion happen in a liquid. Put a glass dish on top of a piece of graph paper. Fill the dish with cold water and let it settle. Now add a drop of food colouring to the water. Time how long it takes for the drop to spread out and cover a particular number of graph squares.

Repeat the experiment with warm water. Does the diffusion happen slower or faster?

OTHER MIXTURES

All kinds of materials form mixtures. Smoke, for instance, is a mixture of hot air (a gas) filled with tiny pieces of soot (a solid). Mist or fog is a mixture of a liquid (tiny water droplets) in a gas (air). Foam is a mixture of a gas in a liquid. The gas is trapped in the liquid and forms bubbles.

Fire fighters use foam to put out petrol fires. The foam covers the fire like a blanket, whereas water would make a petrol fire spread. For more about burning, see pages 18–19.

These fire fighters are using foam to blanket the flames of a petrol fire and put them out.

WHICH LIQUIDS MIX?

Pure alcohol is a colourless liquid just like water. If you mix water and pure alcohol, the result is a colourless mixture. Liquids that mix easily like this are said to be miscible. Some liquids do not mix easily – they are said to be immiscible. Oil and water are like this. They do not really mix together – one liquid forms tiny droplets in the other. This kind of mixture is called an emulsion.

MIXING OIL AND WATER

Stir a tablespoon of cold cooking oil into a beaker of water. Can you make an emulsion?

What happens to the mixture after a few minutes?

SOLUTIONS

A solution is a mixture of a liquid with a solid or a gas, in which the solid or gas mixes in completely and seems to disappear (it dissolves). The liquid part of a solution is called a solvent. Water is the most common solvent.

STIRRING IN SUGAR

Set up two beakers of warm water. Put a teaspoon of sugar in each beaker but stir only one beaker. Does stirring help the sugar to dissolve? If it does, you will still see sugar crystals in the unstirred liquid, while the sugar in the stirred liquid will have dissolved.

HELPING FISH BREATHE

Gases can form solutions, too. This is very important for fish and other water creatures. It means that oxygen from the air can dissolve in water. This makes it possible for fish to 'breathe' underwater.

In aquariums, there is a danger that the fish will not get enough oxygen because the tank contains only a small amount of water. To avoid this problem, many aquarium tanks have an air diffuser that pumps lots of air bubbles through the water.

SEPARATING MATERIALS

Do you like drinking coffee? If you do, you might use a coffee maker to make it. Hot water and ground-up coffee beans mix together inside a coffee maker, but only a clear brown liquid flows into your cup. The coffee solids have been separated from the liquid. To find out how, read on.

Archaeologists use huge sieves. The soil at a dig is sieved to find small fragments of pottery, small metal objects such as coins, and bones.

SIEVING

A sieve is a fine wire mesh with small holes in it. Large solid particles can be separated from smaller ones with a sieve. Small particles pass through the sieve, while larger ones are left behind.

A sieve can also be used to separate large solids from a liquid. A cook uses a colander (a kind of sieve) to separate pasta from the water it is cooked in.

FILTERING

Filtering is similar to sieving, but in a filter the holes are much smaller than in a sieve.

When a mixture is poured into a filter, the liquid passes through the tiny holes and the solids remain behind. Filters are used in coffee machines to separate the ground-up coffee beans from the water.

EVAPORATION

Sieving and filtering can separate mixtures, but they are no good for separating the parts of a solution. One way to get back a solid dissolved in a liquid is to evaporate off the liquid (the solvent). The solvent escapes into the air, and the solid is left behind.

You can use a large plastic drinks bottle with the top cut off to hold the filter funnel. Ask an adult to cut off the top.

SEPARATING SAND AND SALT

Put some sand and some salt into a beaker of water and stir it up. Pour the mixture through a filter to separate out the sand.

Now put the liquid in a dish on a sunny window-sill and let the water evaporate. You will be left with the salt in the bottom of the dish.

DISTILLATION

When a solution is allowed to evaporate, the solvent is lost into the air. However, sometimes we want to collect the solvent as well as the solid. We can do this using distillation. In this process the solution is heated in a flask connected to a tube that is cooled by water. When the solvent evaporates, it rises up into the tube, but because the tube is cooled, the gas condenses. It then runs into a beaker and is collected.

In some coastal places where fresh water is scarce, sea water is distilled to remove the salt and make it fit for drinking,

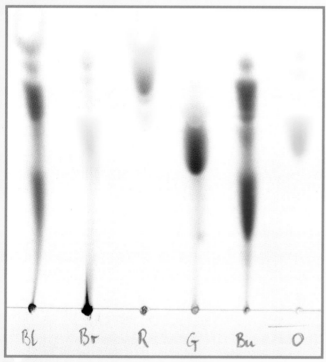

The pigments (coloured chemicals) in several different coloured inks have been separated in this paper chromatogram. From left to right, the pigments are black, brown, red, green, blue and orange.

CHROMATOGRAPHY

Chromatography is a way of separating a mixture of substances in a liquid or a gas. In paper chromatography, a drop of liquid is placed near one end of a piece of filter paper and the end is dipped in a solvent such as water. The solvent rises through the paper, passes through the spot and carries the substances upwards. The substances travel at different speeds in the solvent and settle in different regions of the paper. If the substances are different colours, such as dyes, they can easily be seen.

THE PIGMENTS IN PLANTS

Mikhail Tsvet (1872–1919) was a Russian botanist who wanted to learn more about the pigments (coloured chemicals) in plants. He developed the earliest kind of chromatography, in which he poured mixtures of plant pigments through a column packed with a special powder.

Different plant pigments travelled different distances down the column and formed bands of colours. Tsvet named the process after the Greek word for "written in colour" – chromatography. It has since been used to help separate and identify many other biologically important materials.

CHEMICAL CHANGES

If you stir sugar into water (see page 13) it disappears, seemingly for good. However, it has only dissolved, and it would be possible to get the sugar back by evaporating off the water. But if you put sugar into a biscuit mixture and bake it in the oven, the sugar is changed and you cannot get it back. The baking process is a change that cannot be reversed.

We have seen that all materials are made of tiny particles – atoms or molecules (page 8). When substances are simply mixed, the different particles mingle but do not change. But in an irreversible change such as baking, the atoms and molecules in the mixture interact with each other, and new substances are formed.

Particles might split apart into smaller particles, or they might join up to form bigger particles. These kinds of changes are called chemical reactions.

REACTANTS AND PRODUCTS

The substances that take part in a chemical reaction are called the reactants. The new substances that are produced by the reaction are called the products.

One example of a chemical reaction is between baking soda and vinegar. This reaction produces bubbles of carbon dioxide gas, and it can be used to make a model of an erupting volcano.

AN ERUPTING VOLCANO

Put a tablespoon of baking soda in a small plastic bottle. Put the bottle in a tray of sand and build up sand round its sides in the shape of a volcano. Put a drop of red food colouring into half a cup of vinegar and carefully pour the vinegar into the bottle. Stand back and wait for the eruption.

MAKING CONCRETE

Concrete is a mixture of sand, gravel, cement and water. When the water mixes with the cement, a chemical reaction takes place. The cement changes from a grey powder into tiny crystals. They bind together the sand grains and pieces of gravel to make a strong material used in building.

RUST

The chemical reaction between baking soda and vinegar is fast, but others are much slower. If iron is left in damp surroundings, it gradually begins to rust. The rusting happens because, in damp conditions, particles of oxygen from the air react with particles of iron and form iron oxide. This is the red-brown material we call rust.

A piece of rusty iron on a pebbly beach. Iron rusts even faster in salt water than in fresh water.

HOW LONG DOES IT TAKE TO RUST?

Wrap up some iron nails in a wet paper towel and put them in a plastic bag. Seal the bag, but check the nails every day for signs of rust. Repeat the experiment with two bags of damp nails. Put one in a cold place, such as the fridge, and one in a warm place, like an airing cupboard. Predict which will rust first, then test your prediction.

FROM GASES TO FERTILISER

Chemical reactions do not take place just between solids and liquids – they can take place between gases too. In 1908, Fritz Haber (1868–1934), a German chemist, built some apparatus for making hydrogen and nitrogen gases react together to create ammonia gas. In 1913 another German scientist, Carl Bosch (1874–1940), built a chemical plant (a factory) for making ammonia in large quantities. Ammonia is still made in chemical plants today. Nitrogen and hydrogen gases are heated and squashed together until the reaction takes place that produces ammonia. Ammonia has many uses, including making fertiliser. Part of your meal may have been grown with the help of fertiliser made in an ammonia plant.

17

BURNING

Burning is a spectacular chemical reaction – but it can be dangerous. Large amounts of heat are given out, which can cause other materials to catch fire. And when certain materials burn, they produce poisonous fumes. Burning is a reaction that must be treated with great care.

Materials that burn are called fuels. A fuel usually has to be heated before it will burn, but once it starts burning, it gives out more heat.

A BURNING CANDLE

The fuel in a candle is wax, which is made from hydrogen and carbon. When a candle burns, the wax takes part in a reaction with oxygen that produces carbon dioxide and water vapour. Both the products are gases and mix with the air.

A CAMP FIRE

Many people enjoy a camp fire. Wood is made from carbon and hydrogen, but there are other substances present too. When wood burns, the carbon and hydrogen react with oxygen to form carbon dioxide and water vapour, just as in a candle. But some of the other materials do not burn: they are left behind and form ash. Ash is rich in simple chemicals called minerals. Plants need minerals to help them grow well, so if the ash is added to soil, it will help new plants to grow.

A fire that is out of control can cause great damage and injury.

THE TRIANGLE OF FIRE

A fire needs three things to burn – oxygen, fuel and heat. This is known as the triangle of fire. If any one of these is removed, the fire will go out.

The triangle of fire is useful when fighting fires. Foresters leave wide gaps between stands of trees to stop fires spreading. Trees are the fuel in a forest fire, so if a gap is left, there is no fuel for the fire and it will go out. Fire engines pump water onto a fire to cool it and put it out. Some fire extinguishers produce a foam (see page 13), which smothers fires and prevents oxygen getting to them.

MAKE A FIRE EXTINGUISHER

Set up a candle in a tray of sand. Ask an adult to light it. Pour half a cup of vinegar into a jug, add a teaspoon of baking soda and let the mixture fizz. Carbon dioxide, which is heavier than air, will collect in the jug. Carefully tip the jug so the carbon dioxide spreads over the candle. The carbon dioxide stops oxygen getting to the flame, so the candle should go out.

EXTINGUISHING A THEORY

When wood burns, it leaves only a small amount of ash. For many years scientists wondered what happened to the rest of the wood, which seemed to disappear. Georg Stahl (1660–1734), a German doctor, believed that when something burned, a substance that he called phlogiston escaped into the air. Scientists accepted the phlogiston theory for over a hundred years.

According to the phlogiston theory, all substances heated in air would lose weight. However, experiments showed that some substances actually gain weight when they burn. Antoine Lavoisier (1743–1794), a French scientist, studied these burning experiments and repeated them. His work led to the discovery that when something burns, oxygen combines with the fuel to form an oxide.

When wood burns, the oxide (carbon dioxide) is a gas, and mixes with the air. But other fuels burn to form solid oxides, and the oxygen added to the fuel increases its weight after burning.

Antoine Lavoisier.

ELEMENTS

Imagine that you are an alchemist living nearly 400 years ago. You are looking for a substance called the philosopher's stone, that you believe can give eternal life, and change ordinary metals into gold. You have heated many things, but have not found anything new. In desperation you decide to heat up urine. When the smelly fumes clear away, you find that you are left with a white, waxy substance. When you put it in the dark you are amazed to see that it glows.

This story actually happened – the alchemist was a German called Hennig Brand. He did not find the philosopher's stone, but he was the first person to discover a new element. Brand called the substance phosphorus, which means 'light bearer'.

WHAT IS AN ELEMENT?

There are millions and millions of different materials – too many to count – but there are only just over a hundred elements. Elements are materials made from just one kind of atom.

Elements are the building blocks for other materials. They can combine in a huge variety of ways to form all the other substances that exist. You can find out more about some of the compounds made from elements on page 23.

	1	2	3	4	5	6	7	8	9
1	1 H Hydrogen								
2	3 Li Lithium	4 Be Beryllium							
3	11 Na Sodium	12 Mg Magnesium							
4	19 K Potassium	20 Ca Calcium	21 Sc Scandium	22 Ti Titanium	23 V Vanadium	24 Cr Chromium	25 Mn Manganese	26 Fe Iron	27 Co Cobalt
5	37 Rb Rubidium	38 Sr Strontium	39 Y Yttrium	40 Zr Zirconium	41 Nb Niobium	42 Mo Molybdenum	43 Tc Technetium	44 Ru Ruthenium	45 Rh Rhodium
6	55 Cs Caesium	56 Ba Barium		72 Hf Hafnium	73 Ta Tantalum	74 W Tungsten	75 Re Rhenium	76 Os Osmium	77 Ir Iridium
7	87 Fr Francium	88 Ra Radium		104 Rf Rutherfordium	105 Db Dubnium	106 Sg Seaborgium	107 Bh Bohrium	108 Hs Hassium	109 Mt Meitnerium

			57 La Lanthanum	58 Ce Cerium	59 Pr Praseodymium	60 Nd Neodymium	61 Pm Promethium	62 Sm Samarium	
			89 Ac Actinium	90 Th Thorium	91 Pa Protactinium	92 U Uranium	93 Np Neptunium	94 Pu Plutonium	

John Dalton (1766–1844), an English chemist, studied how elements joined together to make compounds by weighing the elements and the compounds they formed. From his work he found that each element had a particular atomic weight. He decided to arrange the elements in order of atomic weight.

Dmitri Mendeleev (1834–1907), a Russian chemist, noticed that when the elements were arranged in order of atomic weight, elements with similar properties occurred at regular intervals down the list. He arranged the elements into a table called the periodic table, which had elements with similar properties in the same column. Scientists still use a version of the periodic table today.

THE PERIODIC TABLE

Through the studies by Dmitri Mendeleev and others (see panel), scientists realised that elements can be arranged into groups. They can be organised into a table called the periodic table, in which elements in the same group (column) have similar properties. Each element has a one- or two-letter symbol as well as a name. Find out more about these symbols on page 23.

Elements in the same group of the periodic table have similar properties. For example, all the gases in the same column as helium do not react chemically with other elements.

									2 He Helium
				5 B Boron	**6 C** Carbon	**7 N** Nitrogen	**8 O** Oxygen	**9 F** Fluorine	**10 Ne** Neon
				13 Al Aluminium	**14 Si** Silicon	**15 P** Phosphorous	**16 S** Sulphur	**17 Cl** Chlorine	**18 Ar** Argon
28 Ni Nickel	**29 Cu** Copper	**30 Zn** Zinc	**31 Ga** Gallium	**32 Ge** Germanium	**33 As** Arsenic	**34 Se** Selenium	**35 Br** Bromine	**36 Kr** Krypton
46 Pd Palladium	**47 Ag** Silver	**48 Cd** Cadmium	**49 In** Indium	**50 Sn** Tin	**51 Sb** Antimony	**52 Te** Tellurium	**53 I** Iodine	**54 Xe** Xenon
78 Pt Platinum	**79 Au** Gold	**80 Hg** Mercury	**81 Tl** Thallium	**82 Pb** Lead	**83 Bi** Bismuth	**84 Po** Polonium	**85 At** Astatine	**86 Rn** Radon
110 Uun Ununnilium	**111 Uuu** Unununnium	**112 Uub** Ununbium						
63 Eu Europium	**64 Gd** Gadolinium	**65 Tb** Terbium	**66 Dy** Dysprosium	**67 Ho** Holmium	**68 Er** Erbium	**69 Tm** Thulium	**70 Yb** Ytterbium	**71 Lu** Lutetium
95 Am Americium	**96 Cm** Curium	**97 Bk** Berkelium	**98 Cf** Californium	**99 Es** Einsteinium	**100 Fm** Fermium	**101 Md** Mendelevium	**102 No** Nobelium	**103 Lr** Lawrencium
10	11	12	13	14	15	16	17	18

ATOMS AND COMPOUNDS

Look at a ruler and find the millimetre marks. The ruler is no good for measuring atoms but it can give you an idea of how small they are. About 10 million atoms would fit in one millimetre on your ruler.

Scientists used to think of atoms as tiny, hard spheres. They thought they could not be broken up into anything smaller. However, today we know that atoms are themselves made up from smaller particles called sub-atomic particles.

INSIDE AN ATOM

An atom has two main parts. At the centre is a small nucleus, made of particles called protons and neutrons. Moving around the nucleus at high speeds are much tinier particles called electrons.

Electrons have a negative electrical charge and protons have a positive electrical charge, but the number of electrons is the same as the number of protons, so the electrical charges balance. Neutrons do not have an electrical charge.

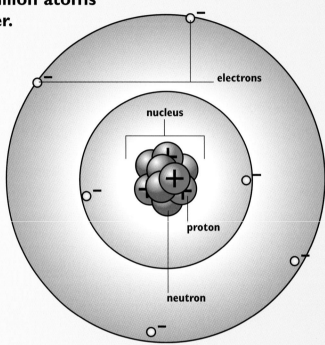

electrons

nucleus

proton

neutron

Different elements have different numbers of protons in their nucleus. Hydrogen has one proton, helium has two, and so on. This coincides with their number in the periodic table (see page 20).

MAKE A SIMPLE ATOM

Ask an adult to cut a large orange in half. Remove the flesh of the orange, leaving two hollow skins. Attach a blob of Plasticine to a fine strand of thread. Using a needle, pull the thread through the top of one of the skins. Let the thread hang down so the end is in the centre of the hollow. Secure the thread to the top of the skin with sticky tape.

The Plasticine represents the nucleus, the hollow is the space inside the atom and the skin represents the outer limit of the atom, where some electrons whizz around. Join up the other half of the skin to make the "atom" complete.

This model of the atom is not to scale. If the nucleus really was this size, the atom would be as wide as four school buses!

COMPOUNDS

Atoms of different elements can join together through chemical reactions to make compounds.

Each element has its own properties. When elements join together to make a compound, the compound has properties that are different from those of the two elements. For example, carbon is a black solid. There is carbon in fuels such as coal and charcoal. Oxygen is a gas that causes things to burn. When coal is burned in air, carbon and oxygen atoms join to make the compound carbon dioxide. This is a colourless gas that does not allow things to burn in it.

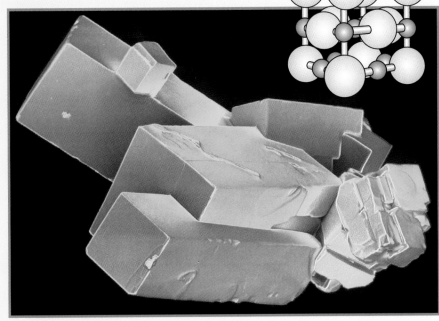

sodium   chlorine

These salt crystals have square shapes. This is because, in salt, sodium and chlorine atoms are joined together in regular cubes (see inset diagram).

TYPES OF COMPOUND

When some atoms form compounds, they stack together in a regular way to make a structure called a lattice. Common salt is a compound like this. It is made from the elements sodium and chlorine.

Atoms can also join together by sharing their electrons. When they do this, they form molecules. Water is made from molecules of two atoms of hydrogen and one atom of oxygen.

When chemists want to record a chemical reaction, they do not draw pictures or write words – they use the symbols in the periodic table on page 20. They use numbers to tell them how many atoms of each element there are in a compound. For instance, carbon dioxide, which has one carbon atom and two oxygens, is written CO_2.

The description of a chemical reaction using symbols is called an equation. The substances on the left of the equation are called the reactants and the substances on the right are called the products.

This is the equation for carbon and oxygen forming carbon dioxide.
$$C + O_2 \rightarrow CO_2$$

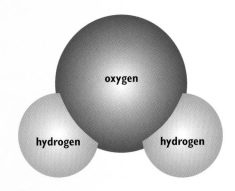

oxygen

hydrogen   hydrogen

The structure of a water molecule. It is written H_2O.

23

ACIDS AND ALKALIS

What do you think of when you think of an acid? The chances are you will think of a dangerous liquid that fumes and can burn your skin. Some acids are indeed like this. Others, such as citric acid, are present in foods, like oranges and grapes.

When you eat a grapefruit, you are swallowing acid! Grapefruit juice contains a weak acid called citric acid.

Alkali is a word you may not have used before. In one way, an alkali is the opposite of an acid. Like acids, there are some alkalis that are safe enough to eat – the baking soda that people use to make cakes rise is an alkali. But alkalis can be just as dangerous as acids. Some alkalis can turn the fat layer of your skin into soap!

HELPFUL ALKALIS

Alkalis are used in the chemical industry to make many useful products. One powerful alkali, sodium hydroxide, is mixed with fats and oils from animals and plants to make soap. Sodium hydroxide is also used in making paper, rubber dyes and bleach. Another alkali, sodium carbonate, is used in making bath crystals and detergents.

ACIDS AND ALCHEMY

Jabir ibn-Hayyan was also known as Abu Musa. His name appears on over 2,000 books, but scholars do not think that he wrote all of them.

Jabir ibn-Hayyan (about 760–815), an Arabian alchemist, used the process of distillation (see page 15) to make a strong acid from vinegar. He also made nitric acid, which is used today to make fertiliser, medicines and fibres for cloth.

Hard soaps are made using sodium hydroxide and vegetable oils. But if you used potassium hydroxide instead, you would get liquid soap.

INDICATORS

Acids and alkalis are often colourless liquids, like water. However, we can tell them apart using substances called indicators. An indicator changes colour when an acid or an alkali is present. The best-known indicator is called litmus paper. There are two kinds. Blue litmus paper is used to test for acids – it turns red when it is dipped in an acid. Red litmus paper tests for alkalis, and goes blue when dipped in an alkali.

A more useful indicator is called universal indicator. It shows a range of colours depending on the strength of the acid or alkali. Strong acids turn it red, weaker acids turn it pink, orange or yellow. Strong alkalis turn universal indicator purple, while weaker alkalis turn it lilac or blue.

A liquid that is neither acid nor alkali is said to be neutral. Pure water is neutral, and turns universal indicator green.

TESTING FOR ACIDS AND ALKALIS

We can use an indicator to test if household materials are acids or alkalis. Wear rubber gloves and safety glasses for this experiment, as some cleaning materials can hurt your skin and eyes.

Put small amounts of lemon juice, vinegar, baking soda dissolved in water, washing-up liquid, salt dissolved in water, and just plain water in separate plastic cups. Test each liquid with universal indicator paper. Which is the most acidic? Which is the most alkaline? Are any of the liquids neutral?

NEUTRALISATION

When an acid and an alkali are mixed in equal amounts, a chemical reaction called neutralisation takes place. The acidity of the acid and the alkalinity of the alkali cancel each other out. The result is a neutral compound called a salt. The salt we put in food (sodium chloride) is only one of many different salts.

The reaction between baking soda and vinegar (see page 16) is a neutralisation reaction. Baking soda is an alkali (sodium carbonate), and vinegar contains ethanoic acid. When they react together they form the salt sodium ethanoate, plus carbon dioxide and water.

USING MATERIALS

Imagine you are a castaway on a desert island. How would you make your home? You might use driftwood from the beach to make the framework of a hut, then cover the framework with huge palm leaves. You could use 'string' made from the long, twisty stems of other plants to hold the palm leaves in place.

In time, you would probably learn to use other materials such as rocks to make tools, and shells for cups. You would be using materials to survive, as people have done for 2 million years.

NATURAL OR MANUFACTURED

We can divide materials into two groups according to where they come from. If they come from the world around us, like wood, stone or wool, they are natural materials. If they come from a factory, like pottery or metals, they are manufactured materials. When a natural material is used to make a manufactured material it is called a raw material. For example, clay is a raw material used to make pottery.

Pottery is one of the oldest manufactured materials. This small vase was made in Greece nearly two thousand years ago.

METALS

Only a few metals (gold, silver and copper) are found naturally as pure metal. Other metals are found in rocks, combined with other substances. Metal-rich rocks of this kind are called ores. In iron ore, for example, iron is combined with oxygen as iron oxide.

Ores are often heated in some way to separate out the metal. Iron can be separated from oxygen by heating it in a blast furnace. Crushed iron ore is tipped into the blast furnace along with coke and limestone. Jets of very hot air heat everything up. The coke burns strongly and the carbon atoms in it combine with oxygen from the air to make carbon monoxide. This gas takes part in a chemical reaction with the iron oxide to make carbon dioxide, leaving behind iron metal.

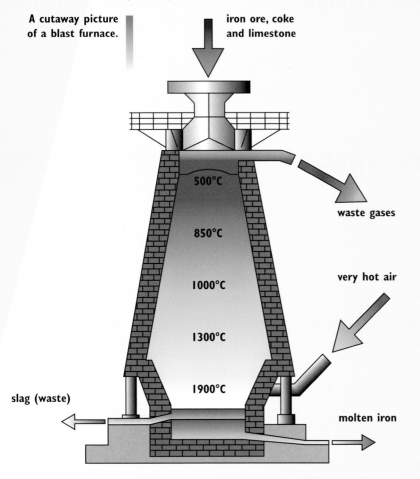

A cutaway picture of a blast furnace.

iron ore, coke and limestone

500°C

waste gases

850°C

very hot air

1000°C

1300°C

1900°C

slag (waste)

molten iron

Iron from a blast furnace is not pure: it contains large amounts of carbon. A more useful material can be made by removing most of the carbon. To do this, oxygen is blasted through the hot metal. The oxygen combines with the carbon to make carbon dioxide and carbon monoxide. The metal that is produced is steel. Steel has a very wide range of uses, from car bodies to paper clips.

An oil refinery. Many of the tall structures are distillation towers where the different chemicals in oil, called hydrocarbons, are separated.

PLASTICS

Plastics are among today's most useful manufactured materials. They are usually made from oil, which is a mixture of hydrocarbons. A hydrocarbon is a chain of carbon atoms with hydrogen atoms attached.

The different hydrocarbons in oil are separated by a special kind of distillation at an oil refinery. To make plastics, small hydrocarbon molecules are joined together into long chains. Sometimes other elements are added as well; for instance, PVC (polyvinyl chloride) contains the element chlorine.

PAPER-MAKING

Paper was invented in China just over 2,000 years ago. It was originally made from hemp plants, which were mashed up in water then laid out on mats to dry. Later, the bark of the mulberry tree was used. Today we use the fibres from wood to make paper. We also recycle paper by mashing it up and using it again.

MAKE RECYCLED PAPER

Cut some paper into short, narrow strips. Mash up the strips with water to make a pulp. Put a thin layer of pulp on a piece of fine wire netting or a metal grid with small spaces (for example a cooling tray for baking). Use a rolling pin to squeeze out some water, then leave the pulp to dry. How does it compare with manufactured paper?

CHEMICALS IN THE ENVIRONMENT

If you look around, you will find chemicals everywhere. You see everything around you through a gaseous mixture of chemicals – the air. Your chair may be made of metal and plastic, or wood and fabric. If you are outside, you may be sitting on grass or stone. All of these are made of chemicals.

It is not only non-living things that are made of chemicals. Plants, animals and you yourself are like living chemistry sets. Almost everything around us is taking part in chemical reactions.

BODY CHEMISTRY

Your body is made from a great many compounds and elements that keep you alive. Your bones are made from calcium compounds and your muscles are made from protein. Your stomach produces a strong acid that kills germs and helps to break down food. And a slimy chemical, called mucin, stops the acid from burning the walls of your stomach.

Chemicals produce the energy you need to do things, and they are used up as the body grows and repairs itself. To replace the chemicals that are used up, we eat food. If you eat a balanced diet you will supply your body with all the chemicals it needs to live healthily.

The chemical reactions that keep you alive produce wastes that you must get rid of. For example, carbon dioxide is a waste that is released when you breathe out.

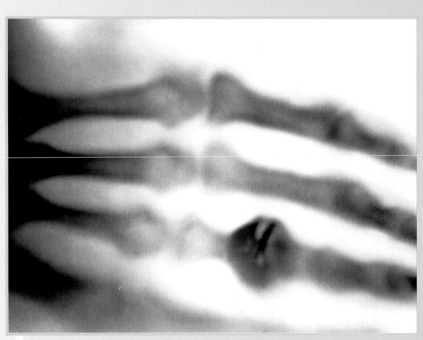

Calcium is an important chemical for the body. If there is too little calcium in your diet, your body takes some from your bones, which may become weak and brittle. This X-ray shows the bones in a hand, one of which has been damaged by disease.

HOW WET ARE YOU?

A human body is about 65 per cent water. To find out how heavy the water in your body is, weigh yourself, divide the answer by 100 then multiply by 65.

ENVIRONMENTAL DAMAGE

We use materials from the environment to make useful objects such as chairs and computers. We also use fuels such as coal, oil and gas to heat our homes or to generate electricity at a power station. Collecting these natural materials can cause environmental damage. For example, we cut down forests for wood to make paper or for building, and we dig huge holes in the ground to mine metals and coal.

We also damage the environment when we burn fuels or turn raw materials into manufactured materials. For example, chemicals such as soot and sulphur dioxide may be released into the air when fuel is burned in a power station. The sulphur dioxide can then dissolve in falling rain and make the rain more acidic. Acid rain and soot can damage living things and destroy habitats.

The older, larger trees in this forest have been badly damaged by acid rain. Slowly, new trees are growing beneath them and the forest is regenerating.

TESTING THE RAIN

Paint a piece of wood white and let the paint dry. Next time it rains, put the wood outside for half an hour then examine it for soot particles with a magnifying glass. Is there soot in the rain? Collect some rainwater in a bowl and use universal indicator paper to test its acidity. Rain is usually a very weak acid, but pollution can make it more acidic.

Many areas of rainforest have been cut down for wood, or to make space for farming. In some areas workers are trying to restore the forest.

ARE MATERIALS RUNNING OUT?

Some materials, such as wool and wood, are renewable. When you shear a sheep it grows more wool, and when you chop down some trees you can plant seeds that will grow into new trees.

Materials such as metals and oil are non-renewable. There are certain amounts of these materials on Earth and, in time, they will run out. To prevent this happening, materials such as paper, metals and glass are being recycled so that fewer supplies have to be taken from the Earth.

Recycling materials can save materials for the future and reduce environmental damage. But we still need to do more to prevent raw materials from eventually running out.

2 million–5500 years ago, the Stone Age. People did not know about metals at this time. Axes, knives and other tools and weapons were made from stone.

3500–2500 BC, the Bronze Age. Bronze (a metal made from tin and copper) was discovered, and many tools and weapons were made from it.

2500 BC–500 AD, the Iron Age. Iron, which is much stronger than bronze, began to be used for making tools and weapons.

Note. The time of the Stone, Bronze and Iron Ages varies from place to place. In the 20th century some rainforest communities still followed a Stone Age way of life.

about 2000 BC, alchemy began in Egypt.

Thales (642–546 BC), a Greek philosopher, thought that all matter was made from one element.

Empedocles (about 490–430 BC), a Greek philosopher, declared that matter consisted of air, earth, fire and water.

Democritus (470–380 BC), a Greek philosopher, thought that matter was made up from tiny particles called atoms.

Jabir ibn-Hayyan (about AD 760–815), an Arabian alchemist, made nitric acid.

Robert Boyle (1627–1691), a British scientist, believed that an element was something that could not be broken down into simpler substances.

Georg Stahl (1660–1734), a German doctor, put forward the phlogiston theory, which said that burning materials gave out phlogiston into the air.

Antoine Lavoisier (1743–1794), a French scientist, showed the phlogiston theory to be wrong and proved that when materials burned they combined with oxygen from the air.

John Dalton (1766–1844), an English chemist, discovered that each element had an atomic weight.

James Clerk Maxwell (1831–1879), a Scottish scientist, developed the idea of matter being made from particles. With Ludwig Bolzmann (see below), he used this idea to explain the behaviour of gases.

Dmitri Mendeleev (1834–1907), a Russian chemist, devised the periodic table of elements.

Ludwig Boltzmann (1844–1906), an Austrian scientist, developed the idea of matter being made from particles. With James Clerk Maxwell (see above), he used this idea to explain the behaviour of gases.

Fritz Haber (1868–1934), a German chemist, made some apparatus in which hydrogen and nitrogen gases could form ammonia gas.

Michael Tsvet (1872–1919), a Russian botanist, invented chromatography.

Carl Bosch (1874–1940) a German scientist, built a factory in which ammonia could be made from hydrogen and nitrogen.

GLOSSARY

acid – a liquid that turns blue litmus paper red. Lemon juice and vinegar are weak acids. Some acids are dangerous and can burn the skin.

adapting – changing something so that it can perform a useful purpose.

alkali – a liquid that turns red litmus paper blue. Baking soda is an alkali, but some alkalis are dangerous.

atoms – very tiny particles that make up all materials.

condensation – a process in which a gas cools down so much that it turns into a liquid.

diffusion – a process in which the particles of two gases or two liquids mix together without being helped (without stirring).

distillation – a process in which a solution is separated and the liquid or liquids that make up the solution are collected.

electron – A tiny particle in an atom that has a negative electrical charge.

element – a substance formed from one type of atom.

Chemical reactions cannot break down an element into a simpler substance.

emulsion – a mixture of two liquids, one of which forms tiny droplets in the other.

evaporation – a process in which a liquid changes into a gas.

habitat – the place where a plant or an animal lives.

hydrocarbon – a molecule made from hydrogen and carbon atoms.

immiscible – a property of a liquid that prevents it from mixing with another liquid.

matter – the 'stuff' that everything is made of: anything that has mass.

miscible – a property of a liquid that allows it to mix with another liquid.

molecule – a group of atoms joined together.

neutron – a particle in the nucleus of an atom that does not have an electrical charge.

periodic table – a table in which the chemical elements are

arranged in order of increasing atomic number (the number of protons in the nucleus). All the elements in the same group or column in the periodic table have similar properties.

philosopher – a person who thinks about things and who uses reason and argument to explain his or her surroundings.

proton – a particle in the nucleus of an atom that has a positive electrical charge.

solution – a liquid in which other substances are dissolved.

solvent – a liquid capable of dissolving a substance.

state – a condition in which matter exists (solid, liquid or gas).

vibrate – to move rapidly from side to side or up and down.

water vapour – water in the form of a gas in the air.

INDEX